Whatever
You Love
You Are

Also by Shelley Townsend-Hudson

Books:

When I Smoked Pot with My Daughter:
  Poems About Parenting
When I Got Drunk with My Mother:
  Poems About Growing Up Southern
Companions for the Soul (with Robert Hudson)

Chapbooks:

When I Got Drunk with My Mother
Into
From the Window
This Southern Thing About Shoes
Paths Before We Knew Them
Hibriten

Whatever You Love You Are

Poems About the Rest of Life

Shelley Townsend-Hudson

PERKIPERY PRESS / CHAPBOOK PRESS
2026

Chapbook Press

Schuler Books
2660 28th Street SE
Grand Rapids, MI 49512
(616) 942-7330
www.schulerbooks.com

Whatever You Love You Are: Poems for the Rest of Life

Published in association with the Perkipery Press.

ISBN 13: 9781966196624
eBook ISBN: 9781966196631

Library of Congress Control Number: 2026904345

For inquiries, contact the author at:
      Perkipery Press
      8405 Baileau Oaks Dr. NE
      Ada, MI   49301
      hudsbob@comcast.net

Most of these poems are new, though some have appeared in these chapbooks:
Hibriten (2004), Paths Before We Knew Them (2005), This Southern Thing About
Shoes (2006), From the Window (2007), Into (2008), and When I Got Drunk with My
Mother (2010), all available from the Perkipery Press.

Cover design by Mark Sheeres

To Robert Hudson

Introduction

This book is a sequel to my two previous collections, *When I Got Drunk with My Mother: Poems About Growing Up Southern* and *When I Smoked Pot with My Daughter: Poems About Parenting*. These new poems were written in many seasons of growth and circumstance, which is why it's subtitled *Poems About the Rest of Life*.

The title, *Whatever You Love You Are*, is a phrase attributed to Jalāl al-Dīn Rumi, the thirteenth-century Sufi mystic who taught that love shapes identity. The things you continually return to—emotionally, mentally, spiritually—form you. For me, this idea pertains to my passions, what I enjoy doing that makes the hours pass like minutes. Not that I want time to pass quickly at this stage of life, oh, no! In fact, I've often felt that pictures, images, and memory are ways to hold on to time, to expand it, preserve it, and slow it down. I love memories from childhood—and I'm blessed with many, and my memories of my children and husband are some of the richest I have—a source of dopamine and serotonin. And I do like my dopamine and serotonin!

On the day Bob and I were married he presented me with a chapbook of songs he'd written for me. One entitled "The Angel Song" (no, not about me) is about Bob asking God to make him into a true and loving person; the chorus goes, "Can you make me, Lord, into an angel? An angel would be very nice. It would be very nice." Bob was then, and still is, a person who thrives by thinking on good things. He lives authentically, true to his passions, always making intentional efforts toward being aware of what he loves.

When Rumi wrote, "Whatever you love you are," he prefaced it with the phrase "It is a subtle truth." Subtle because it is inward-looking. Subtle because it implies a profound, internal shift. By loving something, you actively cultivate those qualities within yourself. If you love music, there is music in you. If you love compassion, you have the capacity to be compassionate.

May these poems be a mirror that reflects something already alive in you. May they be little breadcrumbs leading you back to your essence, to your joy-filled, childlike, original self.

—Shelley Townsend-Hudson

Old Salem, NC, February 2026

Whatever
You Love
You Are

Prologue: On Reading the Poet Laureate

I read Billy Collins late last night
and laughed and slept and in my dream
wrote long lyrical run-ons,
not good ones, but once I rolled
over and thought, not half-bad

Next morning I looked for the lost line;
looked in the title of a CD, on a magazine
cover, it had nothing to do with the coffee
stain on a napkin or pink half-kiss
on the mug, or the phone ringing only once

While driving, images rose and fell
from the windshield, the smiling
tree-fork, a crow leaning into the wind,
that little wooden cross by the guardrail,
which has been altered once again

Objects have adorned it since its
arrival last spring, recently SpongeBob
balloons, now a stuffed white bear,

that little clown of the woods, with blue
plastic eyes and purple satin bow,

soon to grow grey, propped at the base,
reminding passersby a child died
here but is not forgotten, ever,
but remembered in lovely incantatory
enjambments, weaving through dreams

and when it's dawn, the mind, like fresh
blank pages, writes itself anew each day,
lost lines being but a second life—
the door blown ajar, the smell of lilacs,
snow before footprints

1: Original Family

Seventy Times Seven

You know how it is,
    you wake in the middle
of the night and realize you are
your parents. Deny it, go back
to sleep, rationalize—
at least I'm aware of it …
and let the stars reel.

But if you're pacing,
searching for where
earth soars and blue light
slowly closes westward, you're
likely to find it just east
of every extremity you're
trying to hide.
Follow it.

Enter a darker wood where
the veneer of who you thought
you were goes clear through—yes,

they had their influences—but
fit motions decided upon
will quiet the mind.

Kindergarten

When you're an anxious child
the mush pot is hell's fiery pit
I went there, wet my red overalls
and had to go home

Safe in my blue bedroom
I slowly tugged the little pull
down the silver track of my pants
I hate duck duck goose

the puddle around my feet
scraping of chairs, mopping,
giggles, the total disintegration
of five hard years of becoming

Decorum

Nifty was a word of the fifties—so
were *nasty, pus, poop, cripes, H–E–
double-hockey-sticks. Tetanus,* like
polio or *Kotex* were words mothers
uttered that seeped into our blood.

Once spoken, everything fell under
inspection—picked scabs, hands straying
down there, the vile word that rhymed
with duck. Our small minds worked
overtime, filing words with nuances.

We learned taboo words could make
us laugh. Slurs cut deeper than
shit. What was spoken helped in
coping, unclenching *gritty* from *nitty,*
fancy from *free,* and *ill* from *at ease.*

Birthdays

When I turned ten I got Charmin Chatty
and for my eleventh, a sled, shiny and red
at twelve, a sweater, gloves—a slight letdown—
and a diary with a tiny key

My seventh-grade friends threw me a surprise
party. Homemade signs with "Happy 13th,
Smiley!" my new nickname
We swam, played spin-the-bottle,

pairing off to practice kissing,
my "date" and I, in the dark
not daring to move but I was happy
Then changes came so fast

my father broke his foot, later his hip
after that, early onset dementia
Sisters left for college or married
and on my sixteenth my mother

organized a surprise party with friends,
who by then had taken to calling me
"Moody." I laughed a bit at
the card that opened to a little

bag of screws, wires, and bolts
"to build your own car," admired
the already-black mood ring, inhaled
Wind Song, feeling awkward, sad

My seventeenth, friends and I, silly
and giddy, dyed food in the refrigerator:
blue milk, pink cottage cheese, yellow
whip cream, green yogurt

Five months after my father died,
my mother took me to a trattoria where
an accordion player sang "Happy Birthday."
Mortification on my nineteenth

So many birthdays since, over sixty,
love demonstrated to me every time
bliss and pain wrapped together with rich
associations unique to me and treasured

Unlearning

When you're little you take so much to heart:
the flag must never touch the ground
it takes seven years to digest chewing gum
bitten nails stay in your liver forever

A little older you learn the cold war's
not a war, the iron curtain's not
a curtain, matter's not solid
and time is not linear

You begin to disbelieve things:
nothing bad happens if you drop
the spirit stick or say Macbeth
instead of that Scottish play

Our know-nothingness is like
pledging to life's strangeness
where learning happens only
a little faster than the unlearning

where action and certainty are in
balance with doubt and curiosity
and escaping decline for any length
of time is the miracle

A Daylong of Nearly Forgotten Sounds

Old alarm clock's five-alarm bell
A toaster's mechanical clunk
steady hiss of a kettle
spring of the screen door
and slap-dash bang behind me
into the early morning light

On my bike, jack of hearts
spluttering in wheel spokes
Skritch skritch, the neighbor raking
No annoying leaf blowers yet
Another neighbor swashbuckling
with his beat-up metal can to the curb

Wood thrush in the deep quiet
a deer's magnified huff, pileated
jackhammering—sounds not gone
but rarely heard—ch-ch-ch of locusts,
skittering gravel as I brake and the distinct
sound of the kickstand. Home

Family members generate noise:
back-spinning rotary phone, tape
rewind whirr, carpet sweeper swoosh
View-Master click, Kodak flashcube,
manual typewriter tippity tap tap tap
coffee percolating, LP skipping

They just don't make sounds like they
used to. Even a light switch is mute. And yet
with flashlight under blanket, I can still
hear my own breath, my dog snore
flipping through *Mad* magazine, Bazooka
bubble-bursting's just the same

In the Nantahalas

I googled my grandmother, discovering her novel
in academic libraries all over, Stanford, Michigan,
Cornell, copies that sat in our childhood attic
since 1910, still brown-wrapped from the vanity press,
now perched on shelves in places like Cambridge.

We'd dismantled our home in '93, hauling things
to Goodwill, dispensing granny's books at the local
historical society, a book we'd all read, thinking
the title promised more than delivered, snickering
at purple prose.

Yet now the book's a little up-shelf from
Thomas Wolfe. Graduate students analyze its
heightened emotion as a prime example of Romanticism
from a woman's point of view, an idealized portrait
of a difficult life where virtue won out.

My grandmother's visions moved serenely along
without our knowledge. She, quietly, dependably,

watered that which wouldn't bloom tomorrow;
her soft scratchings, persistent, saying something
more than anything we've bothered to say.

White Pocketbook

You handed her her gift
in late September
the flowers on the wall
looking on as God's eyes,
the dog under the bed
us girls, around the foot

As she proceeded to open it,
your longing curved back
like a thing the throat wanted to say
she said she loved it but no sooner
had you left but its color
was all wrong for the season

her words came plain,
barely audible, at first like all
other words, ordinary out of the lips
but later under the rug
that we step around, the dog
sniffs at and digs for

In this sole home movie
with others of its kind
my parents' voices now my own
amnesiac except for times
I meet surprise when I am mild
and this is how we try to love

Mother, Daughter

In front of the mirror
  I said it, a thing I hadn't
heard in forty-odd years:
"Old as Methuselah."

That's what she'd say, clamping
on earbobs before Service League,
when pressures of appearance
or oppressions of tangles became

too much. She never saw
the nimbus rounding
her head, how slightly
below the angels she was,
or how close at hand,
her gift for verisimilitude.

Undertow Head

She never did like my hair
  it was too thin too tangled
too straight too limp too
lifeless too straggly too dark
too much like Daddy's
she never figured the roots
ran too deep either
because she never saw how
they grew in my mouth
entangling my tongue
Perhaps they were numbered
but how would I know? God
never let on how many. Decades
later I'm counting
the grays

My Sister's Christmas Party

(for Joie, 2025)

I came early to help get things in order.
A caregiver guided me to the bathroom,
where she sat beneath the shower.
She raised her face, found mine,
and laughed—a joyful, astonished laugh
like the cry Elizabeth might have given Mary
when recognition flooded her whole being.

We are old, we're no Mary and Elizabeth
but I know the Spirit when I feel it.
She continued laughing as I shampooed
her hair, her face radiant, eyes shining.
In little ways, she's been leaving
us—a word misplaced, a story thinned.
I stay, holding on to what she's dropped.

Decades ago I dreamt of a trumpet
heralding a coming, a brassy bright
call rolling from the rooftop of our childhood
home down to the old woodshed.

The world did not stir, only she and I
with eyes wide with knowing. As if
the sound had always belonged to us.

In the dream, we were together as we
are now, inside that music—inside her laughter
One call, two hearts—holding a secret
the morning was not yet ready to hear.

2: Marriage

Youngest Children Who Are Spouses

Inevitably, original family becomes
superimposed on all relationships.
Even in the backyard, there's
the overachieving flowering plant,
and we're daisies, the simpletons.

Dappled shade is so inviting,
we'd rather spread our quilt, apart,
but the garden needs us.

The sky grows orange and darkens
in the west as talkative guests demand
our tractable selves. But alone,
together, we push deep roots
and repeat our vows, love us love us not.

Exchanges

Pre-wedding ceremony and my mother
turned to my future mother-in-law,
"My daughters always spend Christmas
with me," and already our mutual lives
turned shadowy, suggested by the wedding
photo arriving later—the one with two bristly
mothers in the narthex glaring in opposite
directions amid all the smiling faces

Bad dreams kept coming post-wedding
until from one another we vowed that life
is only our life now forevermore, an encirclement,
bubble, boundary against effrontery.
So when my mother-in-law inquired, "When
do you plan to start a family?" we stood on
solid it's-our-decision ground, while her eyes
flashed wild at being atypically shut down

Our own daughters may or may not exchange
rings and vows, but whatever transpires
we are compelled to make our influence

a good one. At least, by God, on that one
auspicious day! They know their own minds,
and we will admire whomever they choose

Counting

In our dating days he recited Graves on
his twin bed—counting the beats,
slow heartbeats, my head on his chest
watching a breeze turn leaves inside out,
as if a rain might come. But skies were

clear Carolina blue and later we
walked by the Old Well, Davie Poplar,
the Playmakers Theatre, and Silent Sam,
to the Methodist Church to make out on
the front stoop, happy with no thought of

cloudbursts. It was just he and I, young
but not so young as to be naive; we knew
to keep choosing the life we wanted.
In Michigan, every field, forest, and shore,
every baby entering our lives gladdened

our hearts. An angel always watched from
the edges, slowly moving its large white wings

—the beats, steady and sure, and in that
symbolic so poetic place we declared that
no cataclysmic storm would ever rock us

Small Box

Bob met me in the foyer of Manning Hall
with a small box that I opened to find
earmuffs. We were already engaged

and this signified he'd landed the job
in the north country. Straight away
I checked Climates of the States for

the annual snowfall of our new homeplace
Years afterward, Bob stomped figure
eights through deep snow for our little

terrier to navigate, darting full tilt
like a pinball. I learned terms like white-out,
black ice, thundersnow, and lake effect.

Once I saw a snowbow when the sinking sun
broke out, refracting light rather than
scattering it, as in a rainbow. The light shifting its

path as it traveled through snow was rather like
that little box with earmuffs, shifting my life's
course. And don't you know how full of joy I am?

Counter-Storytelling

(Manning Hall, UNC, 1983)

Mourning doves coo outside Dr. Fred's
office in the stately library-science building
I'm at my desk, feeling lucky to be
working at this venerable school.

Bob works on campus too and we meet
daily for lunch at nearby Lenoir Hall; servers
asking, "Kin I hep ya?" Even now, decades
later, we'll ask each other, "Kin I hep ya?"

not because we poke fun, we just love
the cadence, like the coo-ahh of those doves
that were surely heard back in '68 when
Manning and Lenoir became counter-spaces

for protesters against work conditions at Lenoir
Hall. In the Manning foyer a makeshift "soul
food cafeteria" served fried chicken to boycotters
standing against the National Guard.

The library school is now called Information
Science. Lenoir Hall still retains the name of
a white slave owner. Students crisscross those
same spaces. Things change and remain the same.

when we went Skinny-Dipping

We ambled Taylor Street at dusk
hand in hand passing evening
primrose pale yellow petals
unfurled in the dark, so magic
a time, chimes in the heart and his
straight handsome back I followed
through reeds to a pond

stripped down, we eased into slime
dropping to shoulders, the catch of breath
and press of our bodies, my life's life
Since then—over forty years—it keeps
happening: one takes the other's hand,
totally immersed in the right now
aware how quite consciously it slips by

Limberlost

When I read Gene Stratton-Porter's *Freckles*
    at ten in my little North Carolina hometown,
Grand Rapids was a name without a place
and I never imagined I'd end up living there.

But coming to Michigan at thirty
felt like stepping into my own Limberlost,
that in-between place: no longer the self
I'd outgrown, not yet the one waiting ahead.

Now at seventy the marsh still murmurs,
the path still shifts—yet I keep listening,
slowly parting what's limber from what's lost.
In each step, more light, more grace, more home.

Having Nothing to Do with Us

If a patch-up from a grudge
  unraveled or envy spoiled
our mood, or worse, we vented
on someone weaker than ourselves
then guilt bore on us

We spoke of it as we walked
along a boardwalk that ran
the contours of a bog
We longed for something
having nothing to do with us

to unlink the moods' trick
of looping trails in a long line
of accusation. Then we heard it,
a scurrying under the planks three
or four furry paces ahead of us

When we stopped, it stopped,
as if tapping out allegorically
how to shift and resolve

our private experience
Then it un-holed itself at the end

of the boardwalk, a ground
squirrel, watching, tugging us
toward its homely love of decay,
a symbiosis—though

the squirrel was not as dissolute
as we—hinting at assurances
with no immediate answer
save that grace would return
to us unbidden

Found Art

(for Bob)

You pocketed a broken rock on Hilton,
peripheral intrigue. Months later, you found
the other half. What made you bend a second
time? Bound by string, the whole
rock sits on our window ledge.

One night you dreamt of a four-leaf clover
near a coiled snake. The next day you found one
by a garden hose. You who follow whispers, see
the precious in the plain, neglected, and discarded.
Step by faithful step, you find the next.

Glade

(for Bob)

Searching by ear
I heard someone in the green
play the clearest tones
and found this sweet cup

Having known sorrow
letting it have its way
afraid to pour my voice
I drank

Your offer of easier times
even with darkness all
around, I accepted. And gentler
seasons followed

Wherever We Walked ...

Above all, do not lose your desire to walk. Every day, I walk myself into a state of well-being and walk away from every illness. I have walked myself into my best thoughts, and I know of no thought so burdensome that one cannot walk away from it.—Søren Kierkegaard

It brought freshness into our lives
on field trails behind our first apartment
grasshoppers springing the way forward

Our first house, sidewalks steered us along
boxy houses past windows on other lives
we pondered what we wanted for ours

Next our log house with a small pond led
to muskrat, dragonfly, frogs, like Basho's,
plop plopping ahead of our steps

With our first child, then a second, laden
with baby carriers, dog in tow, we walked
Natural Beauty road, a joyous load

We traversed the Great Wall of China
to reach our third child, adopting newness,
entering wilderness, but never lost

Children now gone, we are still renewed
despite closing in on the inevitable fork:
each autumn may be the last autumn

of days that shimmer and drop
each day may be the last day
One of us will trail off, the other

continue to our final home
Each moment the last moment to a
photo finish of two indefatigable walkers

3: Parenting

It's Just the Way It Is

It's one of those days, bored with myself
fretting about the times and thinking of Yeats:
The best lack conviction, the worst, full
of passionate intensity and I'm too much
of both. Reeling shadows of indignant
birds overhead, I worry about our children

we worked so hard to bring into the world
and to keep thriving, knowing we'll have to leave
this earth when they might need us most.
Abandoned baby birds. It's just the way it is
As each age spirals out of control their going
forth depends upon their convictions, not ours

Pregnant with my first child I watched my mother die
Clinging to my husband as if being pulled
through a vortex, the same agony a few months
later, my firstborn pressing up through me, as hope
gave birth in the heart's deep core. My children
will make their way, same as I did. It's just the way it is

Affirmative Action

A mother once said to another:
I've watched how your children
respond to you. You are a good mother

The mother felt competent and solid
and began saying good things to
other mothers and felt kinship

But once she heard a mother say behind
another mother's back: She's too tentative
with her children (whatever that meant)

Now no mother was good enough
her children were doomed
and motherhood, a competition

If you opened the little window
and gave it a shove, all the sky
would come in. There'd be no

nosy neighbors watching. You'd go
to sleep and wake never having to think
who likes you and who doesn't

Not a Good Time

A birthday celebration in Chi-town:
American Girl Store, carriage ride, the top
of Sears Tower, and the Field Museum. But
they balked at dad's one request to visit
the Old Town School of Folk Music. Eye rolling,
whining, back-and-forthing with harsh words

Well-intentioned parents do their best
for these who are at once their children
and their captives (and we, theirs) but the returns
of that day brought more than expected:
A man asked for money on the corner of Monroe
and Kedzie, to which a stressed-out dad barked,

"This is not a good time," as if the man
with blood-rimmed eyes could read a room
His face grew dark, and lunging for a slab
of lumber from a dumpster, he began to chase
us. A taxi whizzed up and whisked us away
while we watched the man fade away

behind us, no longer about our wants or
letdowns, not even our safety but only
the tilted man, who, with his wood plank,
left us with single-minded awareness—even
from the five-year-old birthday girl—
that we had it so good and he did not

Pressed Leaves

In a garden on an island grows a splendid
tree, the Pitch-Apple. A friend and I,
like so many other travelers, stopped
to scratch our names on broad-backed
leathery leaves. "Abbie, Age 10" hangs under hot
sun, on a stem of *clusia rosea*.

We promised to return one day to find
the tree. But a good waft could blow away
our names, new foliage taking their place,
bearing other names. If so, may the Gardener
gather them all for her great fat flattened
book of life with dear Abbie, always 10, inside.

Time-Out for Parents

Give me the box of time
to place the ways we wish
we'd been better parents,
less critical and anxious

times we bit air with
snappish opinions or
hurled heaps of shame

Once, after losing tempers,
we huddled in prayer,
it was awkward and only
a bandage, but the best

we could do. Years ago,
in our log house, we read
and sang to them, no other
place was better than there

They were small. A gaze
or a glance sent minor
messages back and forth,
automatic, full of affirmation

Now we strain sometimes,
stuck, trying for amends
so beautiful and confusing
we need a new way

What if we let them think how
they like? We don't have
to match. It's only a bandage
but the best we can do

4. Wayfarings

Even Here

On a scenic overlook
stood a traveler bent-armed
with cell phone, talking,
her words blown
down a mountain peak
through a veil of mist
winding
down to open space
where an old barn leaned
A hawk winged milk-
white skies,
air sumptuous
enough to overcome
linear time

Always poised
for absolutes,
I assumed the traveler
missed the view,
yet I,

sweeping by at
75 mph,
overlooked deer,
fox, rabbit, heron, and a box
turtle
crossing the road
I used to stop for
to carry to the other
side

Potter's Place

We followed footpaths through fields
around Hilltop Farm. A brawny silence of sun
shone on stone fences all around acres
of England's National Trust

We stopped for tea at a nearby shop,
porcelain Peter, Jemima Puddle-Duck,
Samuel Whiskers, Tom Kitten, lined the windowsills:
still money-makers after all these years

The crusty shopkeeper, who'd known her,
told us Miss Potter gave not a whit for children

We adjusted our spines to the bench outside,
thinking of the 300 painted fungi, her research
for a cancer cure. Scientists of the day, all male,
thought her mad, but, pray tell, who remembers them?

Far better, Beatrix, for you to have dressed small beasts
and to have handed them scripts

At the Pavilion

(Swannanoa Gathering, NC, 2005)

Light throbbed through the skin
of the banjo as the old man lifted it
to his ear and thrummed. The moon
over the mountain swelled in the heat,
and cicadas sung unnaturally loud.
The caller gathered the circle.
Dancers sprang from their cages as if
seeking an altered dispensation;
a craving, there was, and release
in the complexity, spinning and weaving,
and the humid light of the pavilion
held every shadow exactly where it fell.

Sleeping Bear Dunes

(August 2007)

Centuries were represented here
on this bare knob where you and I
walked along surfaces of stability
and change, growth and erosion

From a bleak beginning the living
and dying produced what surrounded
us, the Pitcher's Thistle and Piping
Plover, a flower and bird, struggling

to survive. All motions were love, even
melting ice, a sanctity, as if we were
dreaming back to our own larva where
waiting was prayer. We walked dune

over dune, so sure the lake would be just
over the next rise, grateful for the winds
pulling us along to other horizons
where this one would sometime end

Roadside

Once confined to country roads,
    now white crosses dot interstates, are seen in
subdivisions, and at the corner of Fifth

and Oak, in sumac and delphinium.
Why not whirling-legged Sylvesters?
a better detraction from the silence in the underside

of grass where the child was killed
Why not a stabile with a message of
quantum positive change?—we'll take it

with equanimity and put our trust
in the inevitability and great potential
of change. Black arm bands and covering

clocks went the way of solitary people
walking along railroads at dusk, so what
is it with these altars flying by our

windshields? Why not leave the dead to the dead?
These crosses come at such odd
moments, at unexpected—though not
necessarily blind—turns in the road.

5. Copings, Healings

A Short Soliloquy

Make straight paths for your feet.
As long as you have unhealed
places, you'll not know freedom.
No matter how much discipline
you have or what your doctrine,
you'll always be undermined
by false movements of the mind
and its influences.
In everything proceed on this
assumption: your heart is good.

March 21, 2003 1 p.m. ET

Gatherers, hunters, we were in Wal-Mart,
picking up the news on the air
Coalition forces, sporadic barrage, air alerts, Shock and Awe,
shocking no one here
Ten minutes of gunfire, missile fire, explosions,

and then the noisy dead air followed us,
past towers of China-made shoes,
we inspected the goods, unmindful of
the unwinding of
real time
in Baghdad, smoldering,
checking tags

Permanent Marker

I wrote on my arm, "Be strong, let your heart
take courage," my tattoo for the day.
Tomorrow would be something new.
The e's and o's were little doors to enter,
the B and t's, to climb for better views.

I'd always believed heart and courage
were with me but now I longed for some
new unspeakable word, fresh metaphor,
a leather thong to tighten around my arm.

For we were so small, all of us, and the sun
in a grey sky, we didn't always know
where it was. But it called to everyone,
like sheep by the side of the road.

A marvelously intimate sound
we were sure would tell us we had
to make some horrible sacrifice but, no,
only this: don't play dumb to fear
whatever you love, you are.

Thought-Traffic

(after Rumi)

On the porch we talked of houses
and furnishings, oriental rugs, and
silver as though we'd outlast them

Somewhere a bird squawked
We'd heard it but weren't mindful
of it as it took flight over the trees

Like us, it began as embryo, learning
to find wings by dropping
We draw nearer the edge

—midlife—still taking refuge in things
How to find it? the tattered opening
to hatch out our helplessness

From the Unseen

If you want to say what
Hafez has already said
why write a poem?

To move into invisible
worlds takes finding
your own syllables.

If a butterfly lands on you,
you know not to breathe,
you know what's at hand.

Why have Aaron speak
for you? Retrieve your own
voice from the mountains.

As with the butterfly, lit mote,
sun dog, morning star,
it doesn't take a drunk poet

to capture the moon.
Only Rumi can touch it
with two hands, but descend

into your own ruby mine,
words will rise right-hand
running to the sun.

In Vigil

The dog at my feet thrives
like lilies of the field
while I panic in the dark
unable to find the match
for the candle by the bed

In his brown eyes
grace strikes again
and again, adoringly
as if I'm radiance leaping
from a phosphorous head

Call it projection but who
can say he's not spirit
as believed the Native American
His tags jangle off center—
an ancient sound. He divines

my moves then eases
like molasses to my feet,

draining the bent for bolting
from either of us, in
this patch of sun. To people

who'd fret me down,
to events dancing in fake
importance my eyes are lit
by light found here
in this small brown dog

Dinner Guests

What is it about the overconfident
bearing baskets of proclamations
who unnerve us for several days?

Save your words, just breathe
maybe we've read you wrong.
We don't think of competition
until after you leave, but it lingers.

After a time of thinking about
what we love, how little we need;
peace returns: earned, unearned.

Osteo in the Valley

When the house becomes a valley
I take to the woods, get up,
 stackybones, I say, and hook
my dog on a leash

get out of your ossuary
shuffle through leaves, do
a little soft-shoeing, even snowshoeing,
up and down hills the weight of gravity

the quiet frame, rigid, white, a marvel,
up the hill on two strong legs
that pull me down again
into a sleepy swamp

These bones I'll soon enough leave
as others do. But for now they hold me
up, keep me moving, what else to do?
all for the sake of smiling marrow

Light Speed

Remember how shadows swept your bedroom
walls like scaffolding? Mysterious, though
you learned headlights rounding a corner
by your house scanned your room.

You don't recall all your framework
but something still urges you to the foot
of the bed, recognizing itself and passing
into meaning as you peer out your window.

An essence measures watchfulness like
a speedometer pressed against resistance
to get a reading. Even if you're still, under cover,
you know a sweeping glow's already in motion.

In the Keep of Solitude

Of planners and non-planners
I fell into the second group
preferring days with nothing to do
like Snow Days without even any snow

drifting through days as a child
sitting creekside just to watch currents
or to admire a mare grazing afar or
gazing at swirling snow in lamplight

Imagination was a priory. Inclined to
eschew the clocked path, all that growing
up, bowing to rigors and discipline, instead
forsaking the company of can-doers

to be alone—even now—decades later, with
a dog at my side, vibrant from eye to tail
I've settled into a life with less and less
future ahead yet exceptional in simplicity

walking the Cul-de-Sac

A pink tricycle overturned
abandoned at the foot of the drive
tells a tearful tale

a shiny puddle edged with leaves
reflecting tiny clouds and trees
pleases me because I noticed

the dog furiously circles
leash-hobbles me; his motion
of joy runs the length of his back

we untangle and with fuller grip arch up the hill
sun and dust filter through in those
long ribbons that always catch you off-guard

overhearing a wood thrush
trilling its own brand of magic
I'm reminded that while I journey alone

the off-hand wave from a driver
and my own chin-lift back
these lulls they yield connection

as do other sightings: the silver slug
trail, chicory flowers, tiny oil rainbow,
free-range hens next door

grant me all I need now
visuals, offering themselves
to imagination. So take whatever is given

like, for example, these orange floppy
miss-dig flags I've gathered into
a clownish bouquet

Glasses After Dimming Vision

I broke down, got glasses
and for the first time in a long time
saw remarkable vertical lines
tree trunks and actual leaf shapes

And in the car the horizontal run
of a plank fence rooflines with definite
edges numerals on a speed post
storefronts precise in symmetry

Things only envisioned were now
clear. Only God knew how little I
saw, scales fell from my eyes
and everything was imagery

5: Faith

Believer and Infidel

Our lives take aim for something
from birth: you either believe it
or don't. What convinces?

Best days are when we believe,
the worst, come up full of empty
and both rain on all

Since birth we take in provocation
begin to grow but now
the mirror dims

Change is subtle if not imperceptible,
ever-increasing lines on the face
aren't spelling "we're returning"

And "dignified" fell from fashion;
in a world full of shape, we're
losing ours

But the heart continues to move,
what is it doing but searching
for food? the same provocation

since birth. We came like
an arrow and leave like one,
along the arc, we fly

By Halves

The existence of animals
is not important, what counts
is their meaning, said Augustine.
Who knew what Noah thought,

banging away, while God knows
how many animals paired around
the ship. So what if *Helix Pomatia*
is almost gone; there are still

garden slugs to eat, our souls having
long fled into animals, our last
longing into the gopherwood,
where slime trails have dried.

Who needs them, the lion, the whale,
and bear, for what they stir in us;
they are waiting, waiting for
another Noah, waiting for an ark.

A Sabbath-Day's Journey

I would have lived among the Essenes
in Khirbet Qumran, down by the Dead Sea,
irrigating pomegranate trees, dashing among
cliffs, checking channel by channel

for plugs and leaks, keeping drips at a steady.
After fig picking, I'd take off for the cisterns,
(my job to keep them clean), not resisting
a secret dip, the water being so much more refreshing

than the sea. Stretching animal hides by the baths,
plucking nearly unseen hairs, I'd turn them in the sun
while a scribe bathed, a sign he was preparing,

according to law, to write the holiest of names.
Just before nightfall, I'd top off each scribe's ink,
who, next morning, would bend over the Temple Scroll
that neared twenty-five feet. And lengthening more.

Touch the Sleeve

I have left grey matter at the door
been afraid to know my neighbor
dropped ten percent in the bowl
put faith in the 401K
sworn allegiance to the measurable
honed talents to one-up my neighbor
sung hymns of time management
insisted life had no guarantees
So deep in the well of shadow was I
that sun creeping along the rim
shot glints of light so bright I saw
that whatever comes by way of hope
will find its way by need

Keeping Tract

You are not a rock
so I'll not hand you
spiritual laws from a pocket
with a hole in it

But here's an intuition:
We are loved far
more than we'll know.
How can I share this

since coercive truth
is an oxymoron? You
are not a rock as I am not
the ground beneath you.

Deep listening has a pulse
where great shifts occur
beyond debates about
the door to salvation.

Catch at a Straw

(after Rumi)

A favorite thing was lost
then another and another
until it made no sense
to possess anything

You entered a grieving room
thought it locked, but even
Joseph in the well caught
the smell of jasmine

The essential self was with you,
not the one folded in on itself
from childhood, trusting,
"Those others loved me so."

They desired your best
but left you short-changed.
(Likewise, you did the same to them.)
You can't keep thrusting the head

through the five-sense opening
expecting to find your way out.
The door's unguarded, a voice
comes saying, cross over

into the confluence of question,
answer, question, where shame,
fear, and anxiety reside. Welcome
and treat them honorably.

Dark thoughts, unattractive as
they are, may be the guide bearing
down on you, sublime generosity
coming at you. And if the lights

are working off each other, soft
buffetings may catch you off-guard,
but if we speak of hope, then
off-guard is where to be.

Good-byes

We don't pay respects at open caskets
in my family. So, at the funeral, when
my mother-in-law asked if I'd spoken
to Uncle John yet, I blanched.

Believe not. Already said good-bye to him
at the soda shop in Goshen where I last
saw him. He claimed he couldn't see
a damn thing but sure noticed the Amish girl
behind the counter. Leaning into me, he said,
boy, she's a looker.

Buzz on the Moon

(July 20, 1969)

And opening the little plastic pack
he poured the wine from a vial the size
of his fingertip into a small chalice

In the one-sixth gravity, the wine
gracefully curled up the side of
the cup. The Eagle creaked

Giving thanks for being brought
to the Sea of Tranquility, he ate
the tiny Host and swallowed the wine

The very first liquid ever poured
on the moon, very first food ever eaten:
here too, ever newness, ever sustenance

Some People

Some people I see only in profile
with their air of nonattachment,
joy, emptiness,
flexibility, self-awareness

who would've straightway
recognized Jesus on the road to Emmaus,
while I, by the wayside,
stand ankle-deep in Panic Grass

Unearthing Prayers

We'll never know what Jesus drew
in the sand where the adulteress stood
close to death. A word, a symbol,

stick-gash in the dirt. We see
through glass darkly and grope
with shifting boundaries, still

how warm are our knees in the sand,
sieving grains through fingers,
lifting long-embedded rosaries.

Path to Basho's

Ease comes when you no longer
regard others as gadgets

but visionaries—even with their
less-than-perfect sight—whose affronts

nose-dive like winter warblers
Having mapped your inner

chasms you keep slanting
toward the unseen where

even your musty moods—
heaved on and off like greatcoats—

seem slighter, like forgetting
snow while shoveling

Whole Day

Today was blue sky
strength inside
no shadows

Anxiety free
clear perception
eye and ear

inner hearing
no doubling back
I was as I was

out of the closed-in
into the clearing
of dense grass

where a grasshopper
bent a blade
waving antennae

so fine they cast
no shadow, as
weightless as I

domed by blue
and poised
for vaulting

Epilogue: My Seven Minutes

(for Bob)

In seven minutes after death my brain
like a train, will bear me across miles
of memory. I stare into the night

all across my line of vision
our children run laughing as you
chase them in the old apple orchard,

our log house in the background
and dogs running. The train rattles on
the girls fly down the sledding hill then

coming in, snow caked and pink faced
Wheels shake the roadbed ballast
carrying me to our bedroom steps

We rush into a storm, taut steel
on soft carpet as you enter me like a bolt
Beginning our seven-minute passion

Onward, suddenness of trees, the sea
washed with light as you read *Poems of
Ossian* on Keem Bay while our girls clamber

over rocks, later, they shout, Sheep! Sheep!
being stop-the-car-right-now wild
for Irish sheep. From my Pullman berth

I am not yet ready to sleep. I want to hold
hands through a hundred church sermons,
kiss you at every state crossing, hug twelve times

a day, and with the girls on our bed have
Moonface Candle time. I want barn dances,
Moomintroll parties, play banjo to your fiddle,

hear you sing English country songs
above the churning of pistons slowing slowing
until my seven minutes end and our eternity begins

Acknowledgments

My thanks to the friends and family who helped these poems find their shape, especially Bob Hudson. His many readings, insights, and steady encouragement made the work possible. Thank you, Bob, for your patience and feedback.

Thank you to Mark Sheeres, who drew the beautiful cover, and to Pierre Camy of Chapbook Press, who guided it all through the publication process. I'm deeply indebted to you both.

Finally, I'm grateful to everyone who has traveled with me through the many Limberlosts of my life—family, old friends, and those who met me in new places. This small volume only exists because of your presence and kindness.

About Shelley Townsend-Hudson

Shelley Townsend-Hudson was born in Lenoir, North Carolina. Her father, a small-town attorney, gentleman farmer, and lover of poetry, named her in honor of Percy Bysshe Shelley. Her father was a friend of Thomas Wolfe's at the University of North Carolina in 1919. Shelley's childhood home was on a road called Tremont Circle, which wound around a hill at the foot of Hibriten Mountain, just east of Lenoir.

Shelley is a musician, a dancer, and a multi-award-winning poet. Her poems have appeared in various literary journals and in a series of chapbooks published by the Perkipery Press. Her previous books of poetry are *When I Got Drunk with My Mother* and *When I Smoked Pot with My Daughter*. Shelley sings and plays banjo in the old-time string band Gooder'n Grits, which performs for dances and festivals throughout West Michigan.

She enjoys showing her Welsh Terriers in AKC and UKC conformation classes, barn hunt, Fast CAT, and tracking events.

She is married to author Robert Hudson, and they have three daughters, Abbie, Molly, and Lili. Shelley and Robert split their time between Ada, Michigan, and Old Salem, North Carolina—depending on the weather.